240

HANGMAN

Games

For Adults

L.A BOOKS © 2021

All rights reserved to the author

ISBN: 9798747702677

HANGMAN

Hangman is a paper and pencil guessing game for two or more players.

One player thinks of a word, phrase or sentence and the other(s) tries to guess it by suggesting letters within a certain number of guesses.

We Wish You a lot of fun!

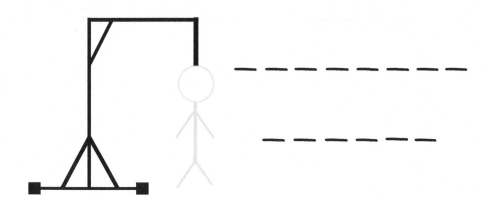

A B C D E F G H I J K L M N O

P Q R S T U V W X Y Z

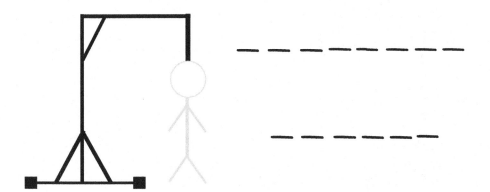

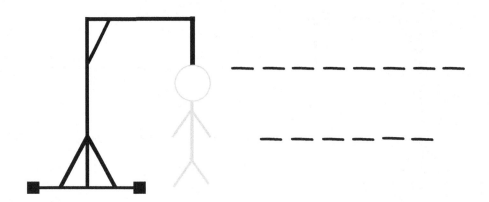

_ _ _ _ _ _ _ _

_ _ _ _ _ _

A B C D E F G H I J K L M N O

P Q R S T U V W X Y Z

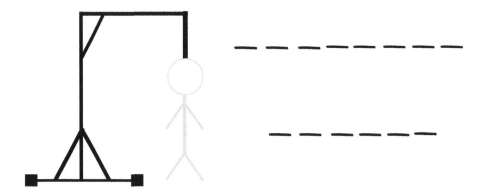

_ _ _ _ _ _ _ _

_ _ _ _ _ _

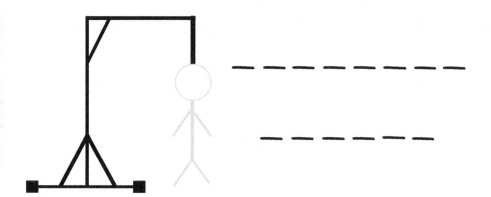

A B C D E F G H I J K L M N O

P Q R S T U V W X Y Z

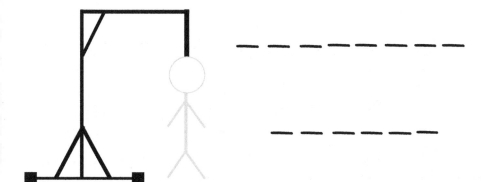

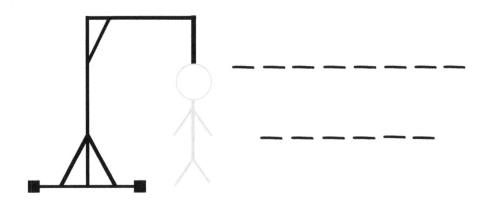

ABCDEFGHIJKLMNO

PQRSTUVWXYZ

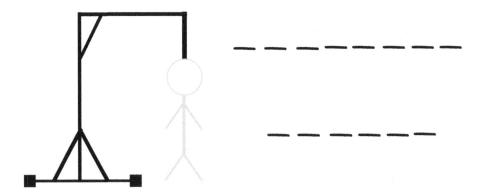

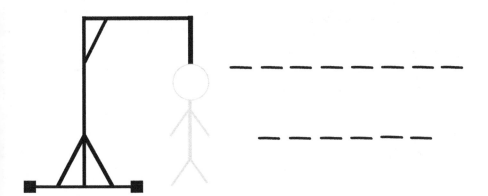

_ _ _ _ _ _ _ _

_ _ _ _ _ _

A B C D E F G H I J K L M N O

 P Q R S T U V W X Y Z

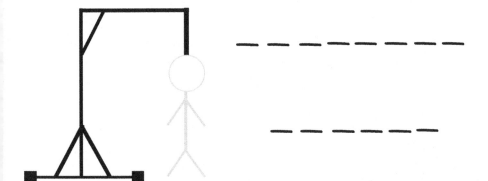

_ _ _ _ _ _ _ _

_ _ _ _ _ _

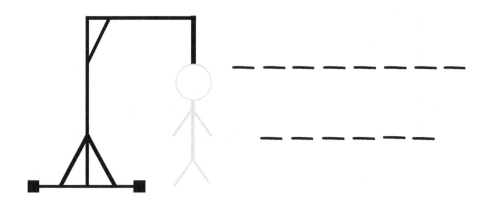

ABCDEFGHIJKLMNO

PQRSTUVWXYZ

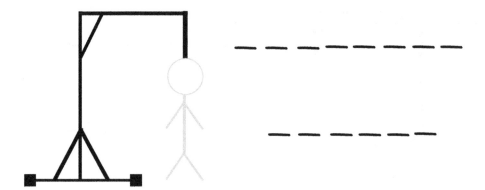

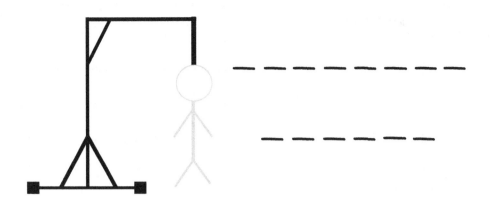

_ _ _ _ _ _ _ _ _ _

_ _ _ _ _ _ _

ABCDEFGHIJKLMNO

PQRSTUVWXYZ

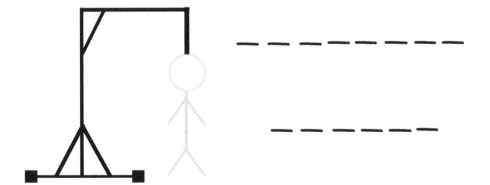

_ _ _ _ _ _ _ _ _ _

_ _ _ _ _ _ _

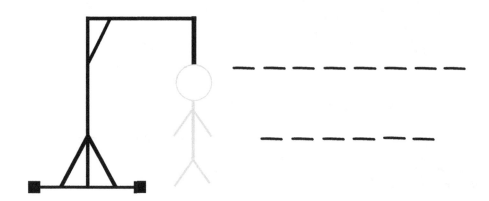

_ _ _ _ _ _ _ _ _ _

_ _ _ _ _ _

A B C D E F G H I J K L M N O

P Q R S T U V W X Y Z

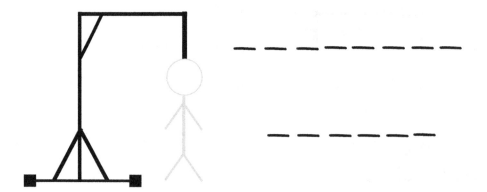

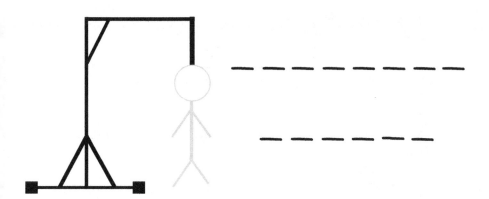

_ _ _ _ _ _ _ _

_ _ _ _ _ _

A B C D E F G H I J K L M N O

P Q R S T U V W X Y Z

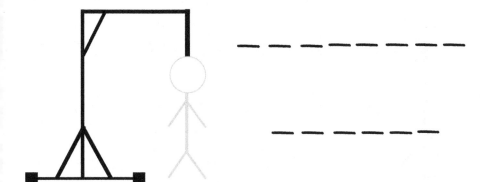

_ _ _ _ _ _ _ _

_ _ _ _ _ _

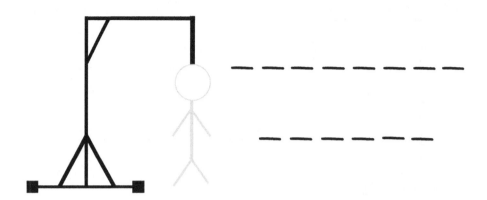

A B C D E F G H I J K L M N O

P Q R S T U V W X Y Z

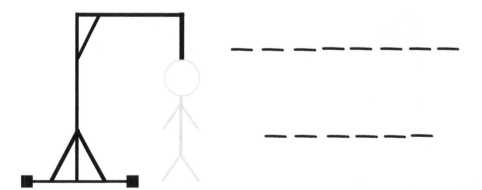

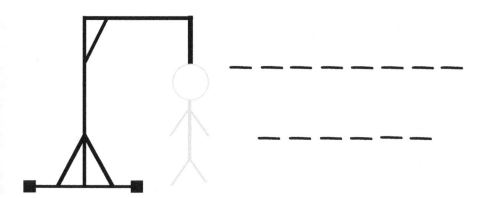

_ _ _ _ _ _ _ _ _ _

_ _ _ _ _ _ _

A B C D E F G H I J K L M N O

P Q R S T U V W X Y Z

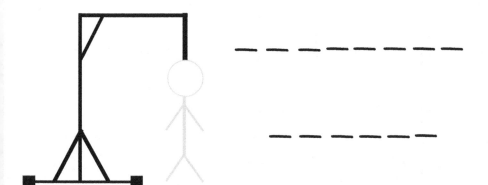

_ _ _ _ _ _ _ _ _ _

_ _ _ _ _ _ _

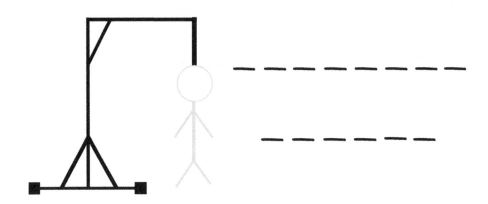

_ _ _ _ _ _ _ _ _

_ _ _ _ _ _ _

A B C D E F G H I J K L M N O

P Q R S T U V W X Y Z

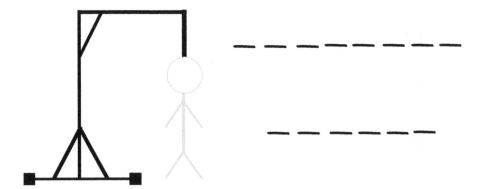

_ _ _ _ _ _ _ _ _

_ _ _ _ _ _

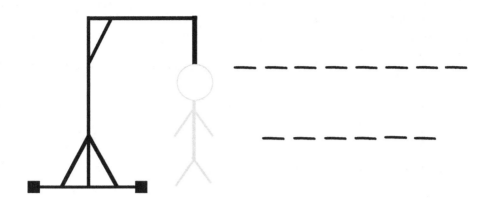

ABCDEFGHIJKLMNO

PQRSTUVWXYZ

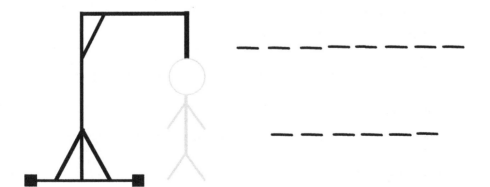

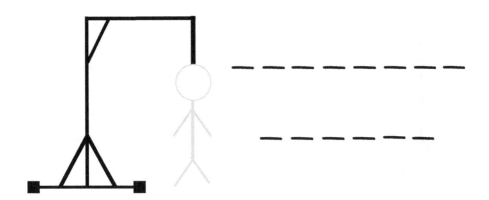

_ _ _ _ _ _ _ _

_ _ _ _ _ _

ABCDEFGHIJKLMNO

PQRSTUVWXYZ

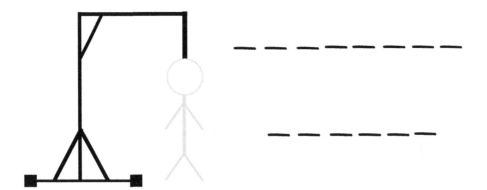

_ _ _ _ _ _ _ _

_ _ _ _ _ _

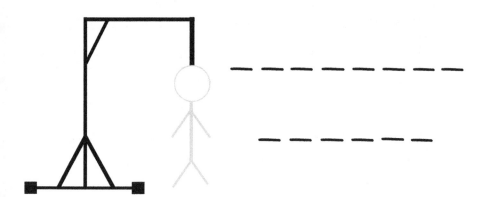

_ _ _ _ _ _ _ _ _ _

_ _ _ _ _ _ _

ABCDEFGHIJKLMNO

PQRSTUVWXYZ

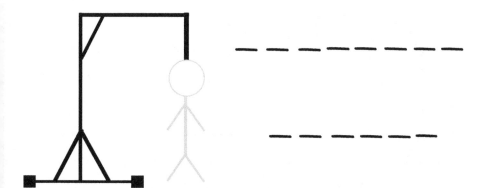

_ _ _ _ _ _ _ _ _ _

_ _ _ _ _ _

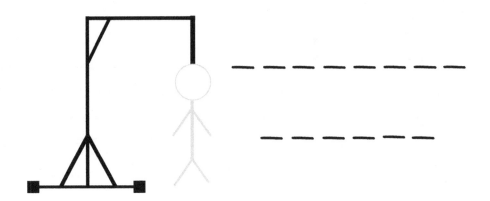

ABCDEFGHIJKLMNO

PQRSTUVWXYZ

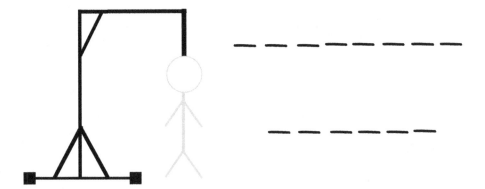

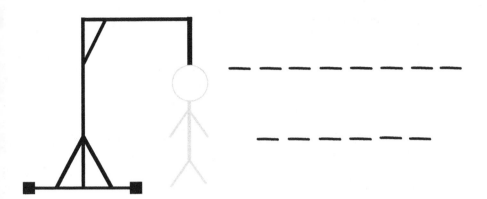

_ _ _ _ _ _ _ _ _ _

_ _ _ _ _ _

A B C D E F G H I J K L M N O
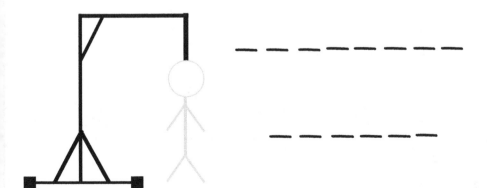
P Q R S T U V W X Y Z

_ _ _ _ _ _ _ _ _ _

_ _ _ _ _ _

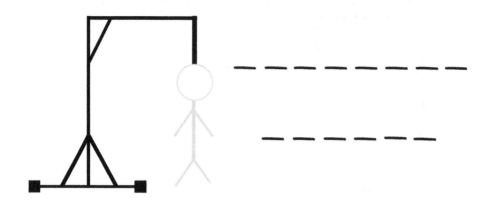

ABCDEFGHIJKLMNO
PQRSTUVWXYZ

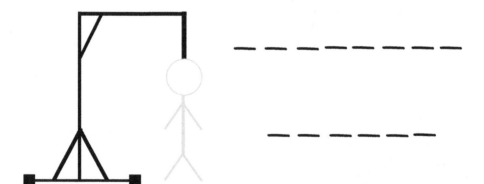

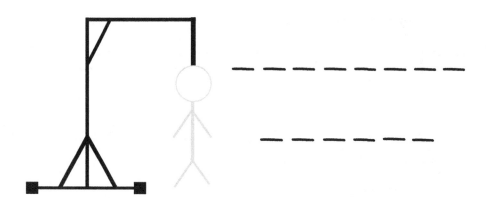

ABCDEFGHIJKLMNO
PQRSTUVWXYZ

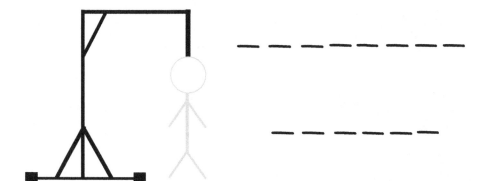

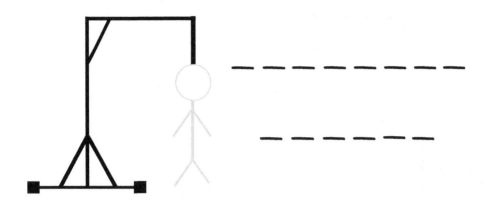

ABCDEFGHIJKLMNO

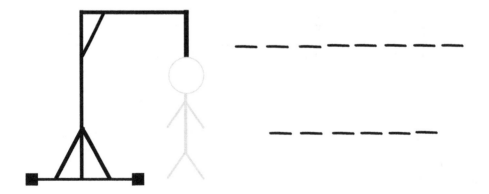

PQRSTUVWXYZ

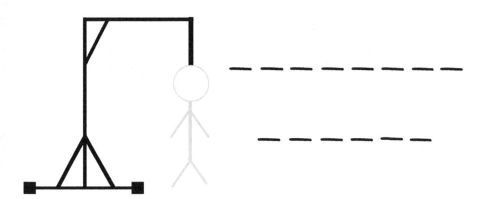

ABCDEFGHIJKLMNO

PQRSTUVWXYZ

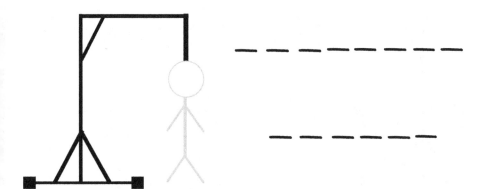

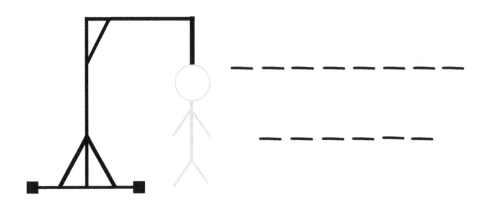

_ _ _ _ _ _ _ _ _ _ _

_ _ _ _ _ _ _

A B C D E F G H I J K L M N O

P Q R S T U V W X Y Z

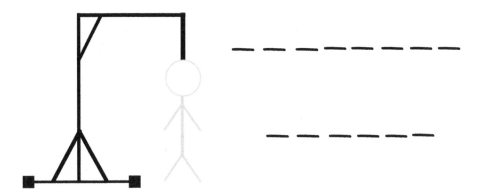

_ _ _ _ _ _ _ _ _ _

_ _ _ _ _

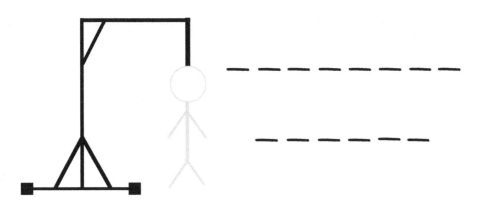

_ _ _ _ _ _ _ _

_ _ _ _ _ _

A B C D E F G H I J K L M N O

P Q R S T U V W X Y Z

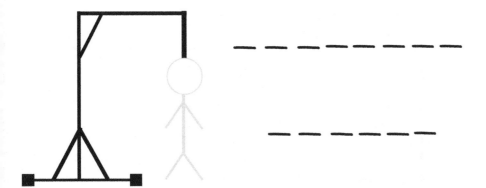

_ _ _ _ _ _ _ _

_ _ _ _ _ _

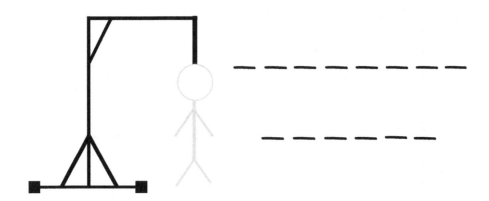

_ _ _ _ _ _ _ _ _

_ _ _ _ _ _ _

A B C D E F G H I J K L M N O

P Q R S T U V W X Y Z

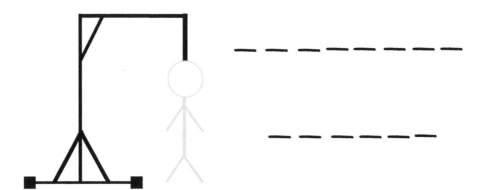

_ _ _ _ _ _ _ _

_ _ _ _ _ _

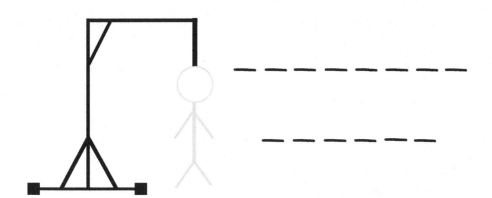

_ _ _ _ _ _ _ _

_ _ _ _ _ _ _

A B C D E F G H I J K L M N O

P Q R S T U V W X Y Z

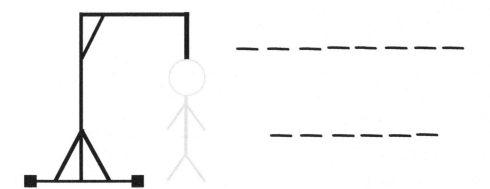

_ _ _ _ _ _ _ _ _

_ _ _ _ _ _

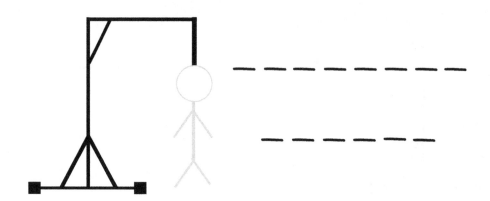

ABCDEFGHIJKLMN O

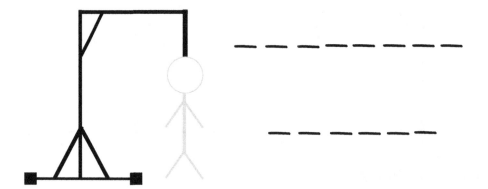

PQRSTUVWXYZ

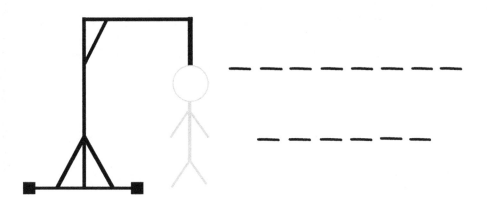

_ _ _ _ _ _ _ _ _ _

_ _ _ _ _ _

ABCDEFGHIJKLMNO

PQRSTUVWXYZ

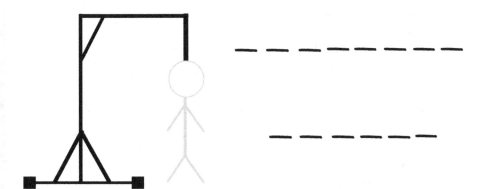

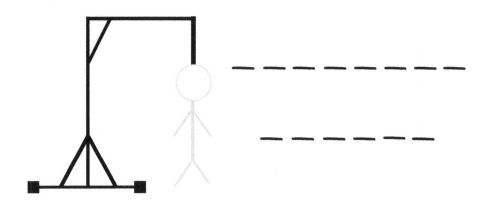

A B C D E F G H I J K L M N O

P Q R S T U V W X Y Z

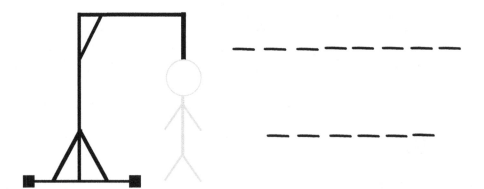

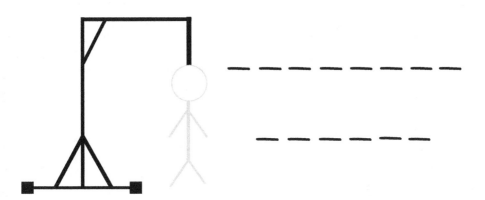

_ _ _ _ _ _ _ _ _

_ _ _ _ _ _

ABCDEFGHIJKLMNO

PQRSTUVWXYZ

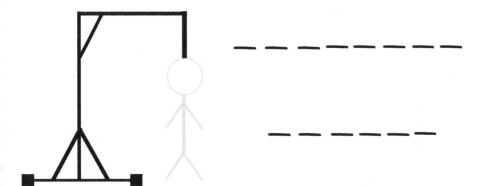

_ _ _ _ _ _ _ _

_ _ _ _ _ _

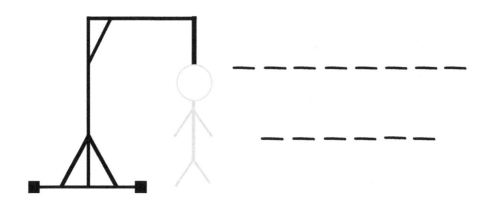

_ _ _ _ _ _ _ _ _

_ _ _ _ _ _ _

A B C D E F G H I J K L M N O

P Q R S T U V W X Y Z

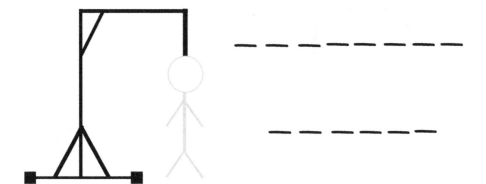

_ _ _ _ _ _ _ _ _

_ _ _ _ _ _

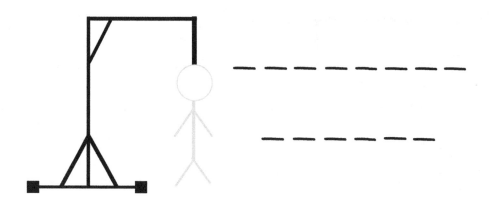

_ _ _ _ _ _ _ _ _ _

_ _ _ _ _ _ _

A B C D E F G H I J K L M N O

P Q R S T U V W X Y Z

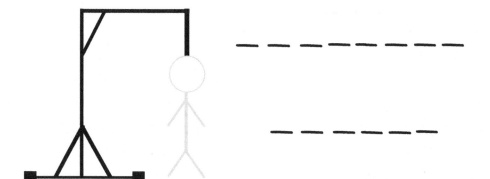

_ _ _ _ _ _ _ _ _

_ _ _ _ _ _

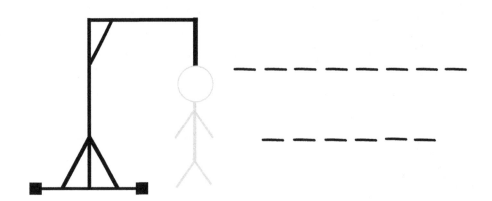

A B C D E F G H I J K L M N O

P Q R S T U V W X Y Z

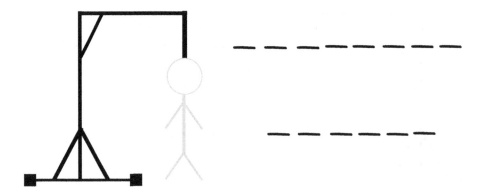

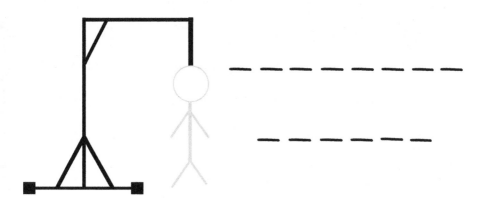

_ _ _ _ _ _ _ _ _

_ _ _ _ _ _

ABCDEFGHIJKLMNO

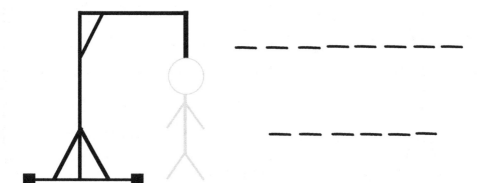

PQRSTUVWXYZ

_ _ _ _ _ _ _ _

_ _ _ _ _

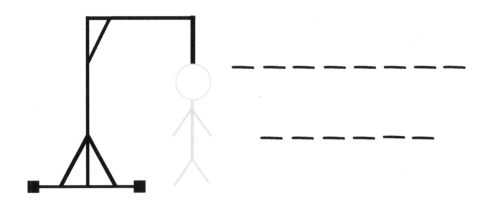

_ _ _ _ _ _ _ _ _

_ _ _ _ _ _ _

ABCDEFGHIJKLMNO

PQRSTUVWXYZ

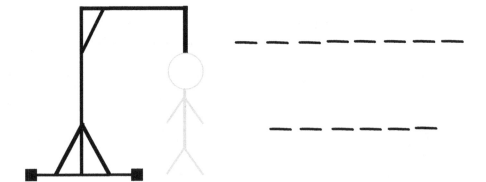

_ _ _ _ _ _ _ _ _

_ _ _ _ _ _

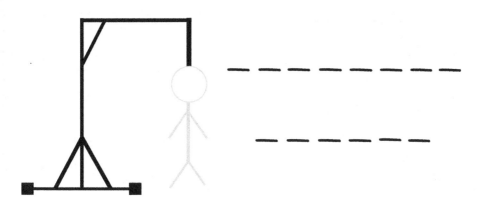

_ _ _ _ _ _ _ _ _

_ _ _ _ _ _ _

A B C D E F G H I J K L M N O

P Q R S T U V W X Y Z

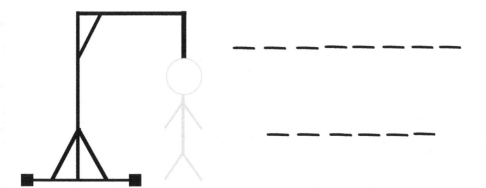

_ _ _ _ _ _ _ _ _

_ _ _ _ _ _

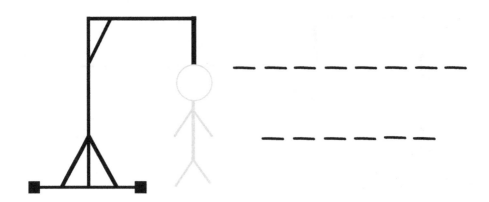

A B C D E F G H I J K L M N O

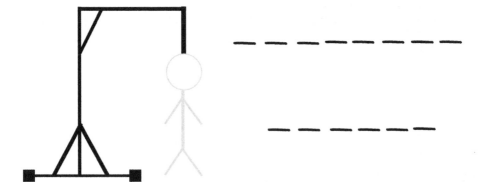

P Q R S T U V W X Y Z

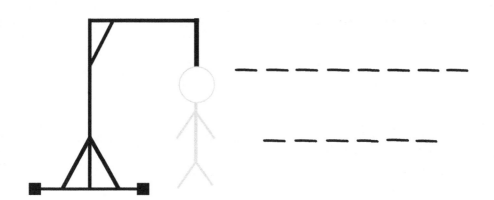

_ _ _ _ _ _ _ _

_ _ _ _ _ _

A B C D E F G H I J K L M N O

P Q R S T U V W X Y Z

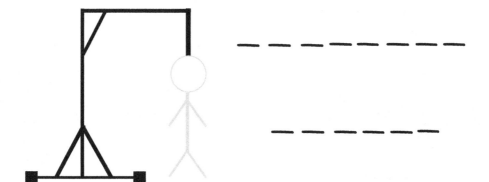

_ _ _ _ _ _ _ _

_ _ _ _ _ _

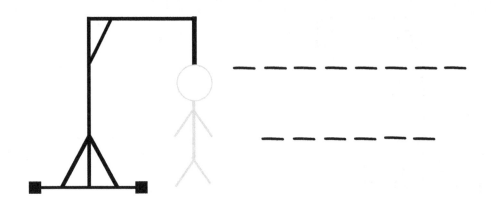

_ _ _ _ _ _ _ _ _ _

_ _ _ _ _ _ _

ABCDEFGHIJKLMNO

PQRSTUVWXYZ

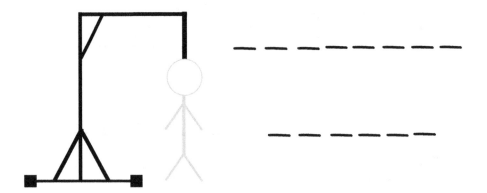

_ _ _ _ _ _ _ _ _

_ _ _ _ _ _

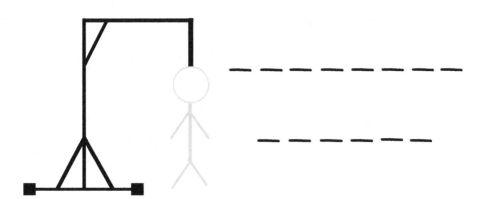

A B C D E F G H I J K L M N O
P Q R S T U V W X Y Z

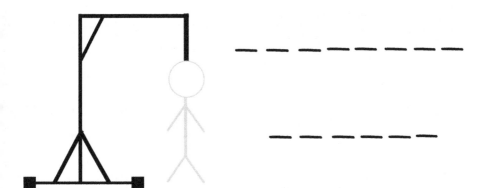

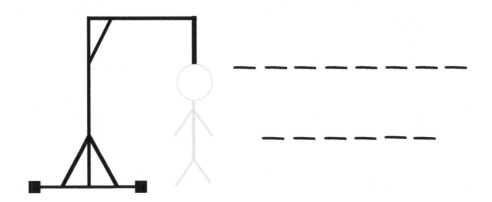

_ _ _ _ _ _ _ _ _ _

_ _ _ _ _ _

A B C D E F G H I J K L M N O

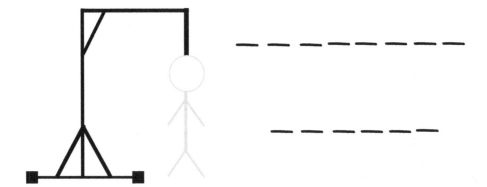

P Q R S T U V W X Y Z

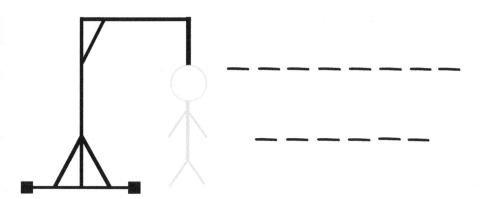

_ _ _ _ _ _ _ _ _ _ _

_ _ _ _ _ _ _

A B C D E F G H I J K L M N O

P Q R S T U V W X Y Z

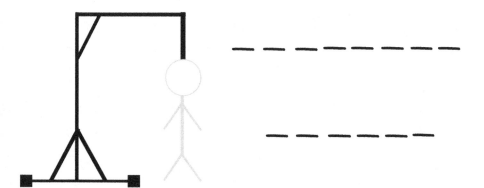

_ _ _ _ _ _ _ _ _

_ _ _ _ _ _

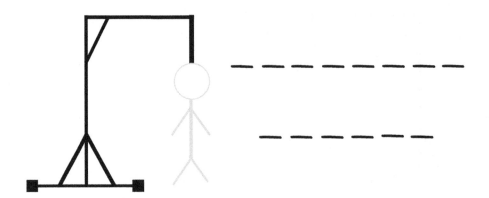

A B C D E F G H I J K L M N O

P Q R S T U V W X Y Z

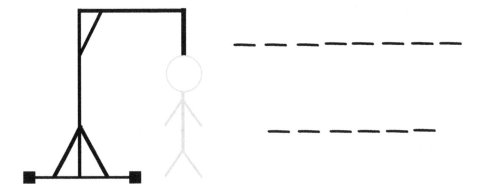

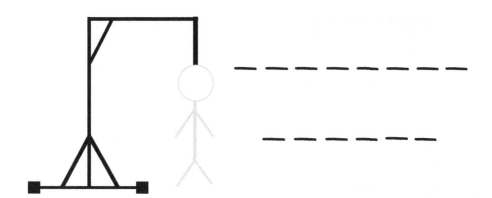

ABCDEFGHIJKLMNO
PQRSTUVWXYZ

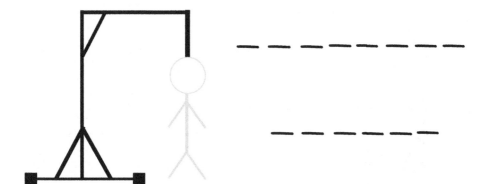

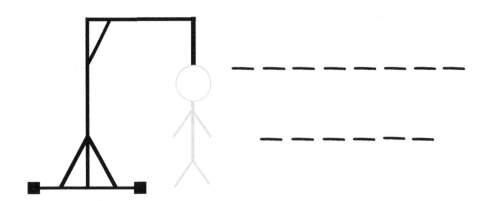

A B C D E F G H I J K L M N O
P Q R S T U V W X Y Z

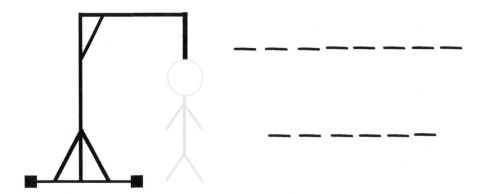

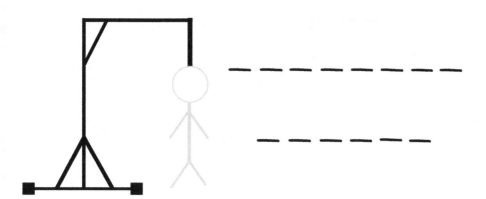

A B C D E F G H I J K L M N O

P Q R S T U V W X Y Z

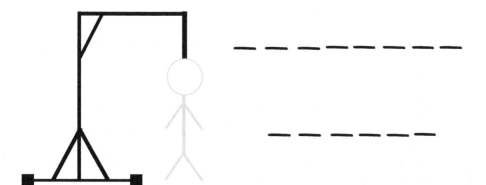

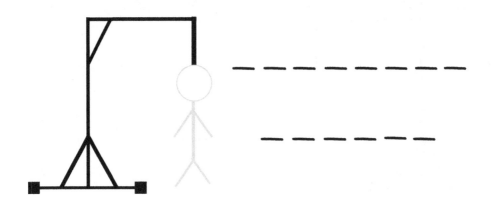

_ _ _ _ _ _ _ _ _ _ _

_ _ _ _ _ _ _ _

ABCDEFGHIJKLMNO

PQRSTUVWXYZ

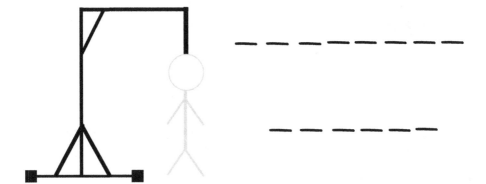

_ _ _ _ _ _ _ _ _

_ _ _ _ _ _

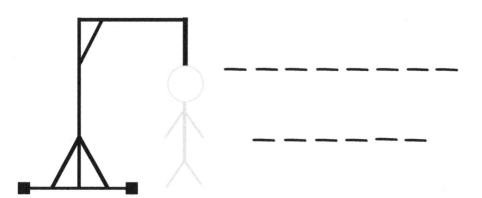

A B C D E F G H I J K L M N O

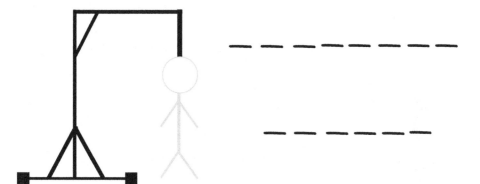

P Q R S T U V W X Y Z

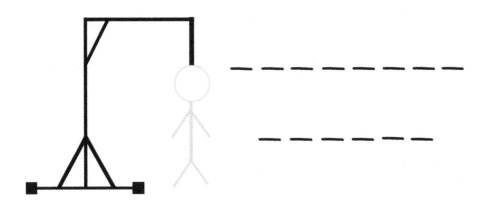

_ _ _ _ _ _ _ _

_ _ _ _ _ _

ABCDEFGHIJKLMNO

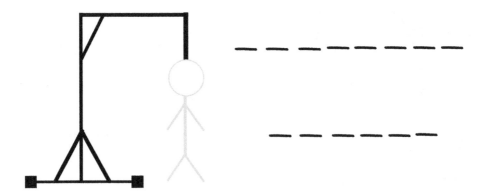

PQRSTUVWXYZ

_ _ _ _ _ _ _ _

_ _ _ _ _

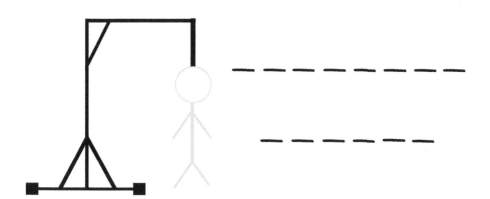

ABCDEFGHIJKLMNO
PQRSTUVWXYZ

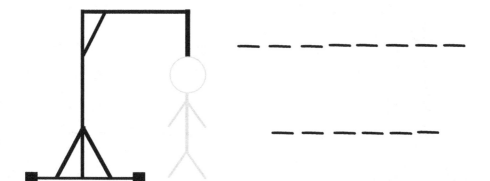

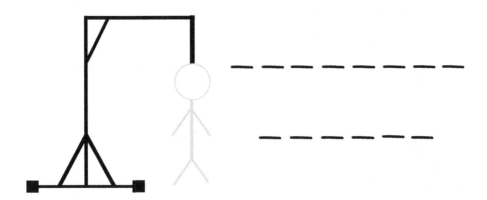

_ _ _ _ _ _ _ _ _

_ _ _ _ _ _

A B C D E F G H I J K L M N O
P Q R S T U V W X Y Z

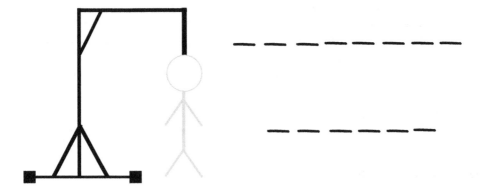

_ _ _ _ _ _ _ _

_ _ _ _ _

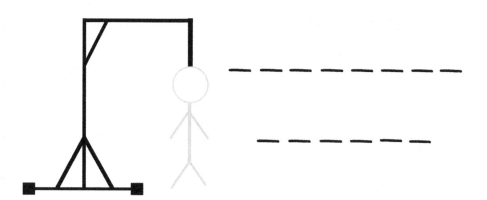

_ _ _ _ _ _ _ _ _ _

_ _ _ _ _ _ _

A B C D E F G H I J K L M N O

P Q R S T U V W X Y Z

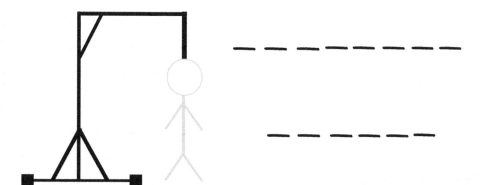

_ _ _ _ _ _ _ _ _ _

_ _ _ _ _ _ _

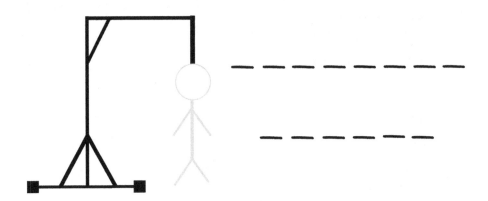

A B C D E F G H I J K L M N O

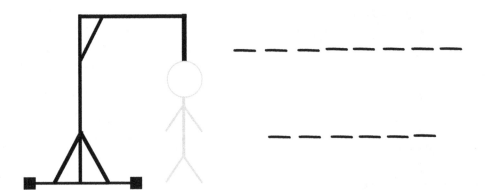

P Q R S T U V W X Y Z

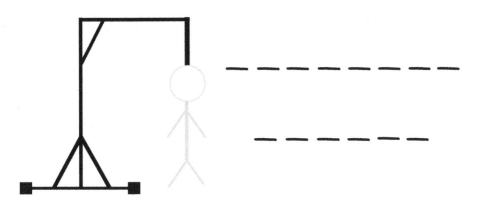

A B C D E F G H I J K L M N O

P Q R S T U V W X Y Z

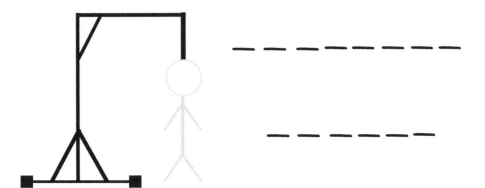

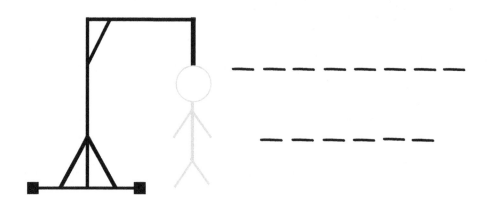

_ _ _ _ _ _ _ _ _ _ _

_ _ _ _ _ _ _

A B C D E F G H I J K L M N O

P Q R S T U V W X Y Z

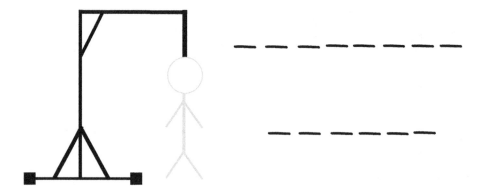

_ _ _ _ _ _ _ _

_ _ _ _ _ _

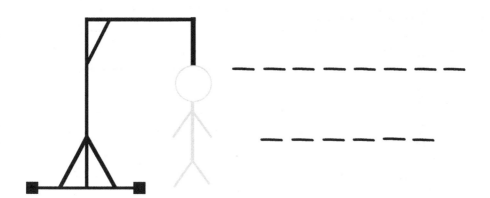

_ _ _ _ _ _ _ _ _ _ _

_ _ _ _ _ _ _ _

A B C D E F G H I J K L M N O

P Q R S T U V W X Y Z

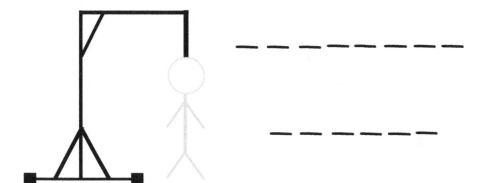

_ _ _ _ _ _ _ _ _

_ _ _ _ _

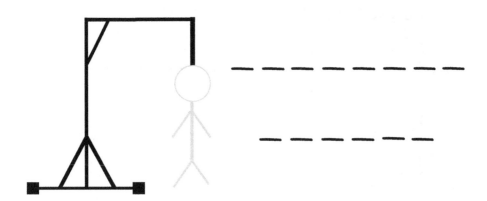

ABCDEFGHIJKLMNO

PQRSTUVWXYZ

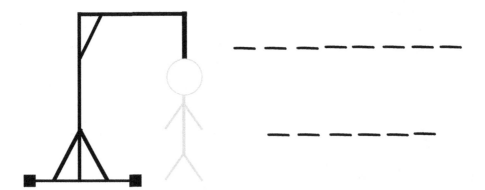

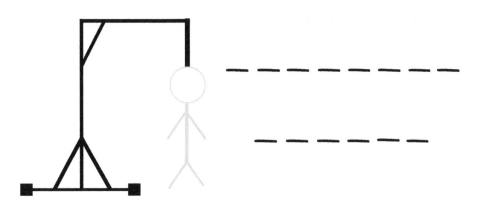

_ _ _ _ _ _ _ _ _ _

_ _ _ _ _ _

A B C D E F G H I J K L M N O

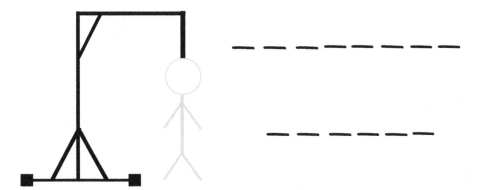

P Q R S T U V W X Y Z

_ _ _ _ _ _ _ _ _ _

_ _ _ _ _ _

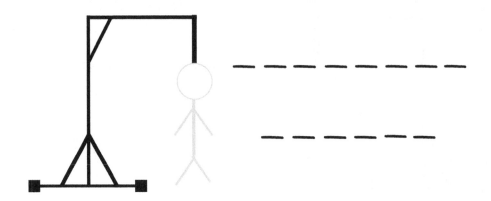

_ _ _ _ _ _ _ _

_ _ _ _ _ _ _

A B C D E F G H I J K L M N O

P Q R S T U V W X Y Z

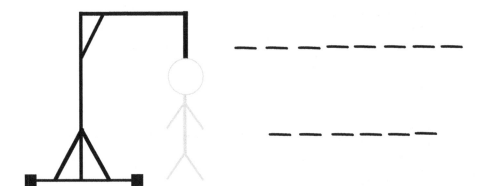

_ _ _ _ _ _ _ _ _

_ _ _ _ _ _

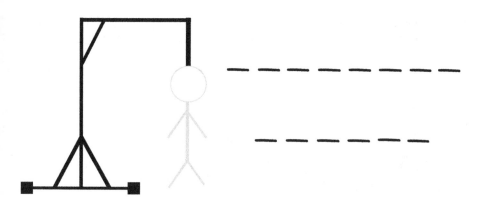

A B C D E F G H I J K L M N O

P Q R S T U V W X Y Z

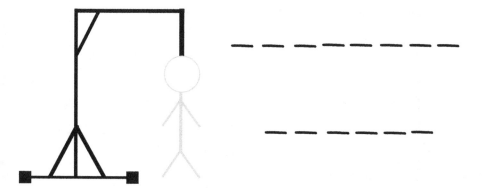

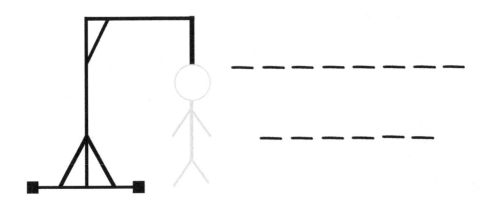

ABCDEFGHIJKLMNO

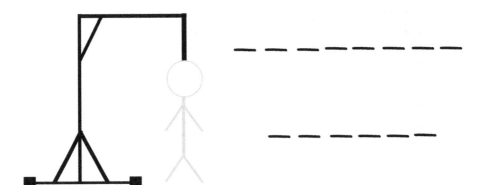

PQRSTUVWXYZ

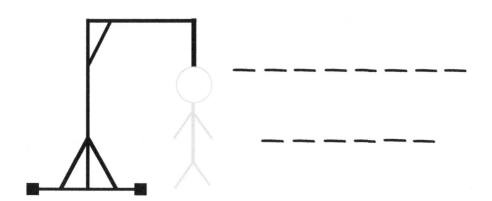

A B C D E F G H I J K L M N O

P Q R S T U V W X Y Z

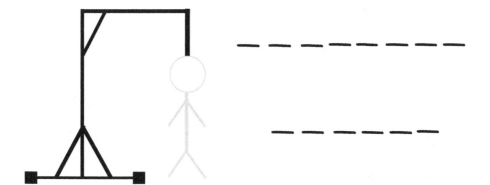

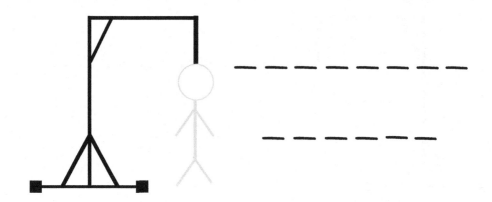

ABCDEFGHIJKLMNO

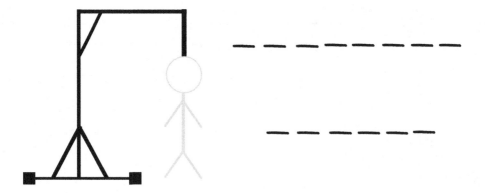

PQRSTUVWXYZ

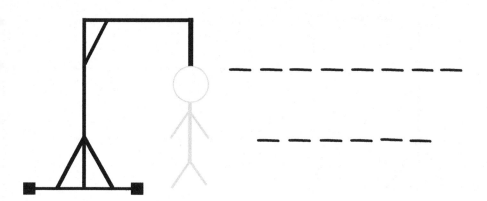

_ _ _ _ _ _ _ _ _ _

_ _ _ _ _ _ _

A B C D E F G H I J K L M N O

P Q R S T U V W X Y Z

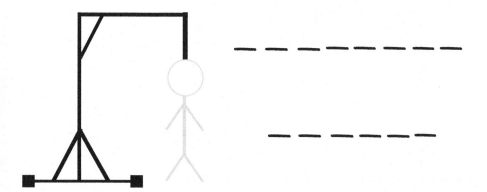

_ _ _ _ _ _ _ _ _ _

_ _ _ _ _ _

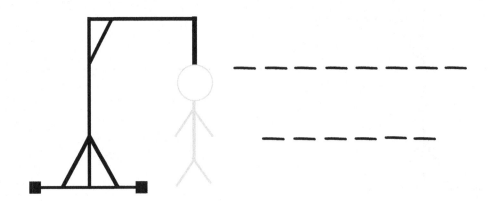

A B C D E F G H I J K L M N O

P Q R S T U V W X Y Z

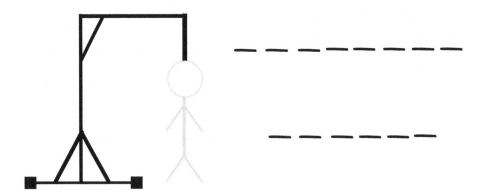

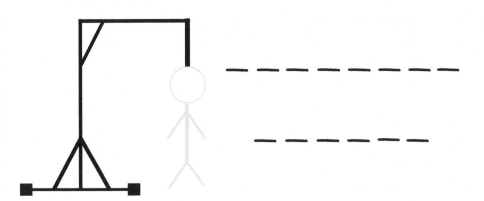

A B C D E F G H I J K L M N O
P Q R S T U V W X Y Z

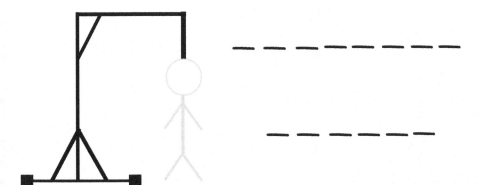

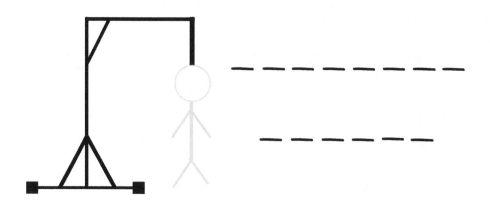

A B C D E F G H I J K L M N O

P Q R S T U V W X Y Z

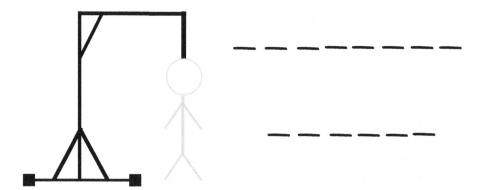

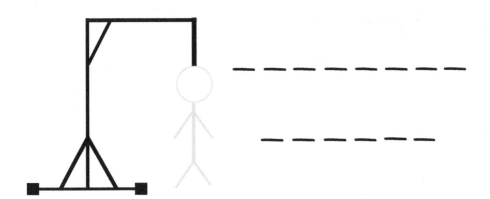

_ _ _ _ _ _ _ _ _ _

_ _ _ _ _ _

A B C D E F G H I J K L M N O

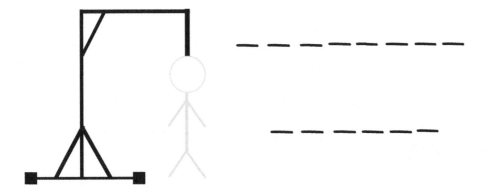

P Q R S T U V W X Y Z

_ _ _ _ _ _ _ _ _ _

_ _ _ _ _ _

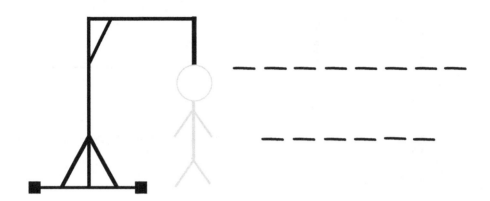

A B C D E F G H I J K L M N O

P Q R S T U V W X Y Z

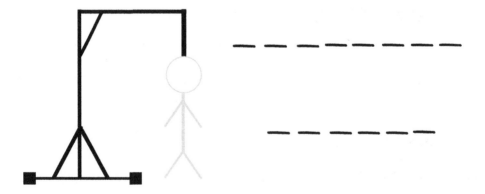

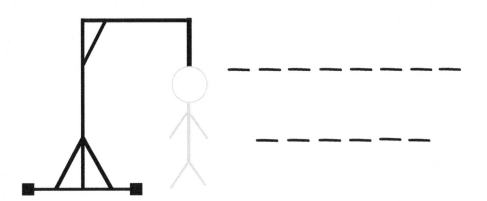

ABCDEFGHIJKLMNO

PQRSTUVWXYZ

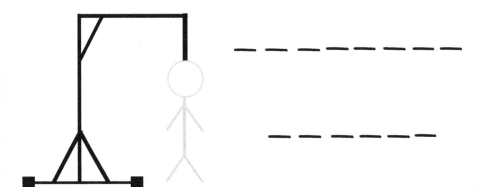

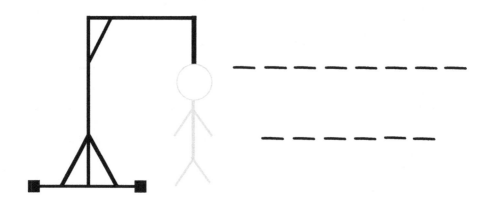

_ _ _ _ _ _ _ _ _ _ _ _

_ _ _ _ _ _ _ _ _

A B C D E F G H I J K L M N O

P Q R S T U V W X Y Z

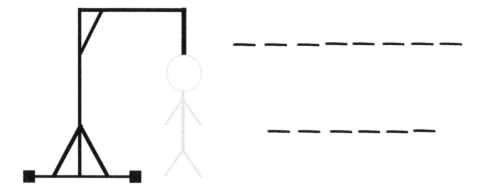

_ _ _ _ _ _ _ _ _ _

_ _ _ _ _ _

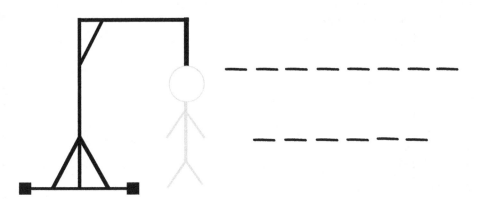

A B C D E F G H I J K L M N O

P Q R S T U V W X Y Z

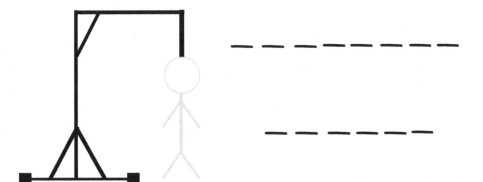

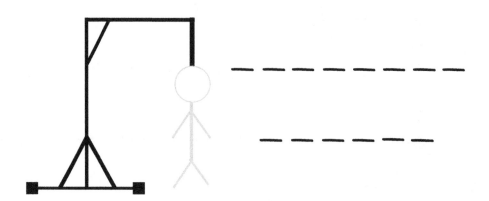

ABCDEFGHIJKLMNO

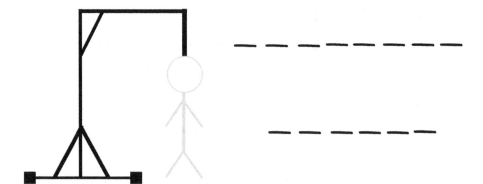

PQRSTUVWXYZ

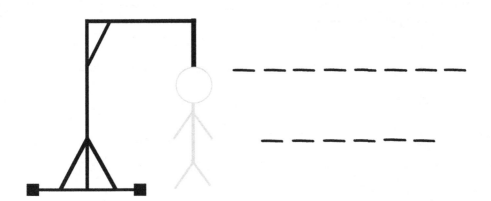

ABCDEFGHIJKLMNO

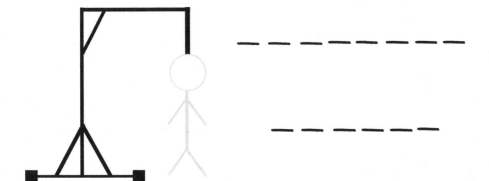

PQRSTUVWXYZ

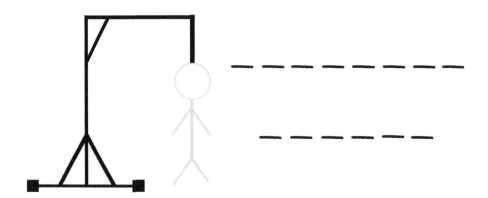

A B C D E F G H I J K L M N O
P Q R S T U V W X Y Z

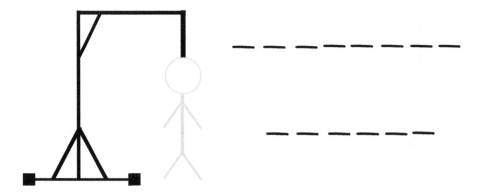

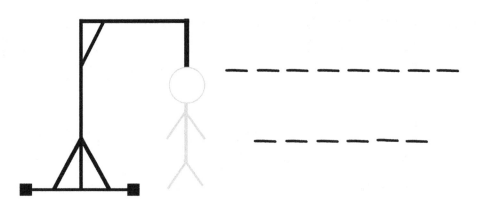

ABCDEFGHIJKLMNO

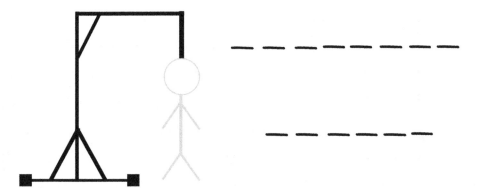

PQRSTUVWXYZ

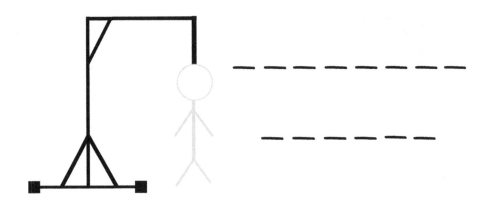

A B C D E F G H I J K L M N O

P Q R S T U V W X Y Z

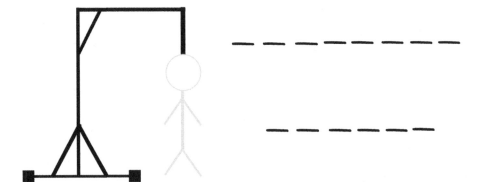

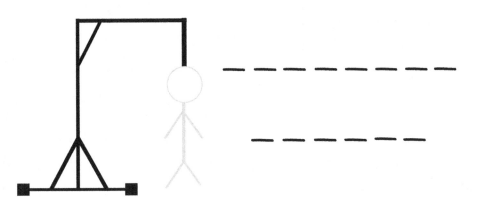

_ _ _ _ _ _ _ _ _ _

_ _ _ _ _ _ _ _

A B C D E F G H I J K L M N O

P Q R S T U V W X Y Z

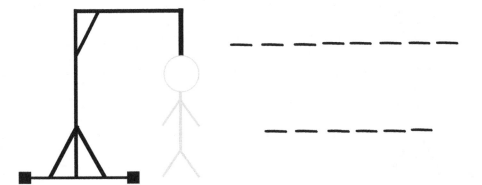

_ _ _ _ _ _ _ _ _ _

_ _ _ _ _ _ _

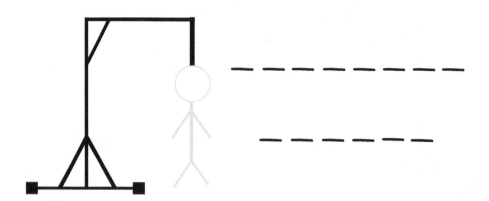

ABCDEFGHIJKLMNO

PQRSTUVWXYZ

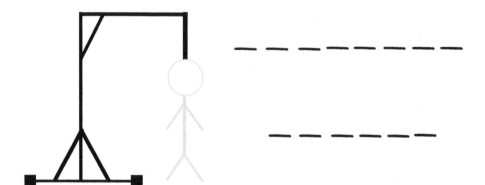

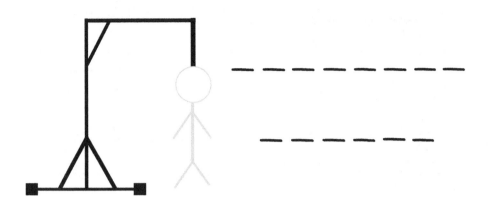

ABCDEFGHIJKLMNO

PQRSTUVWXYZ

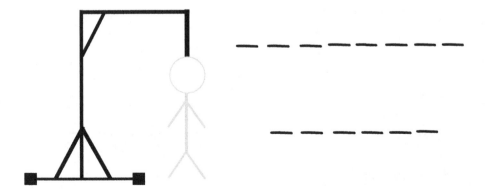

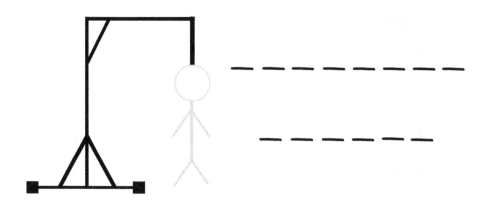

A B C D E F G H I J K L M N O

P Q R S T U V W X Y Z

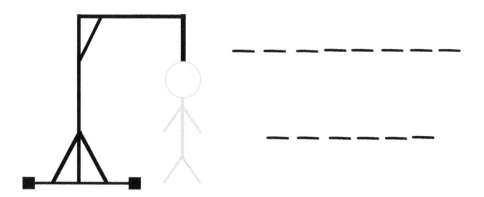

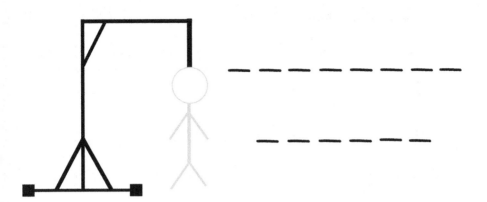

ABCDEFGHIJKLMNO

PQRSTUVWXYZ

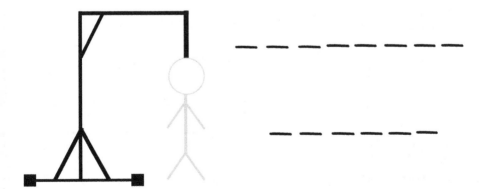

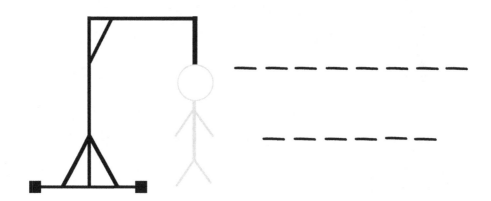

ABCDEFGHIJKLMNO

PQRSTUVWXYZ

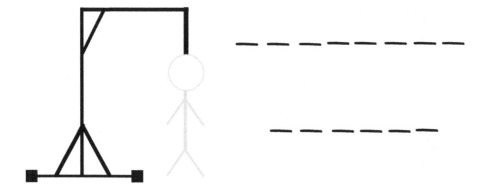

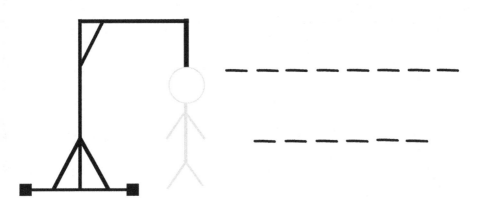

ABCDEFGHIJKLMN O

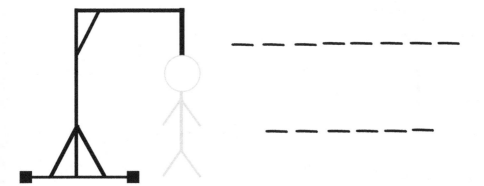 PQRSTUVWXYZ

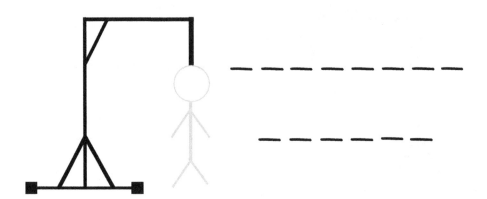

- - - - - - - - - - - - -

- - - - - - - - - - -

ABCDEFGHIJKLMNO
PQRSTUVWXYZ

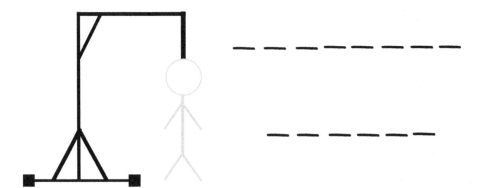

- - - - - - - - - - - - -

- - - - - - - - -

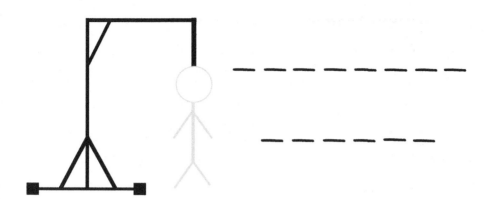

_ _ _ _ _ _ _ _ _ _

_ _ _ _ _ _ _

ABCDEFGHIJKLMNO
PQRSTUVWXYZ

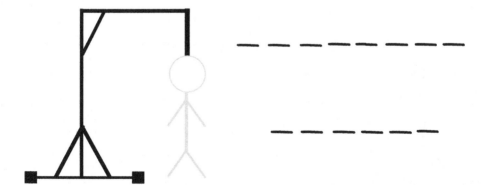

_ _ _ _ _ _ _ _ _ _

_ _ _ _ _ _ _

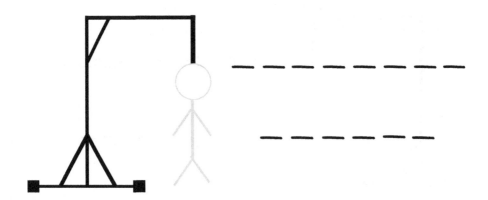

_ _ _ _ _ _ _ _ _ _

_ _ _ _ _ _ _

ABCDEFGHIJKLMNO
PQRSTUVWXYZ

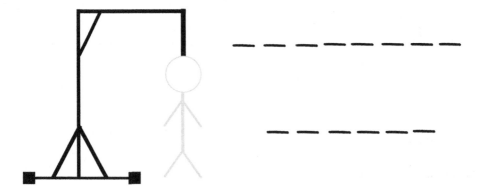

_ _ _ _ _ _ _ _ _

_ _ _ _ _ _

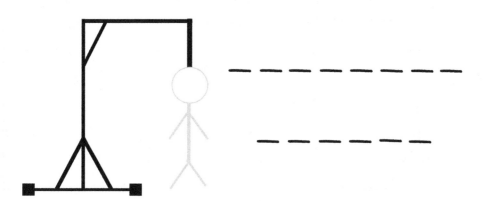

ABCDEFGHIJKLMNO

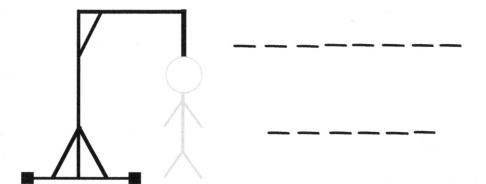

PQRSTUVWXYZ

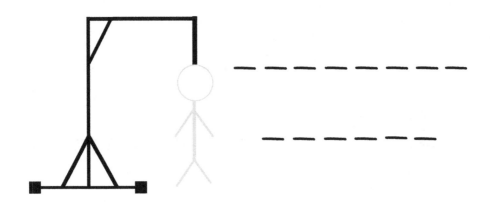

ABCDEFGHIJKLMNO

PQRSTUVWXYZ

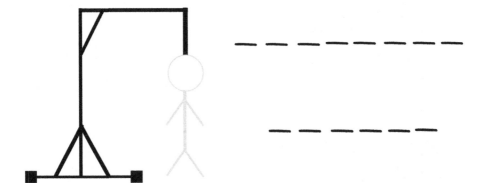

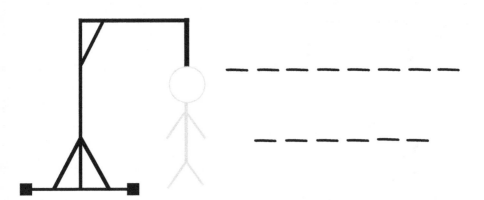

ABCDEFGHIJKLMNO
PQRSTUVWXYZ

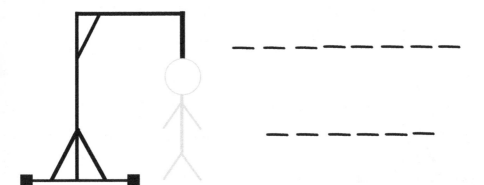

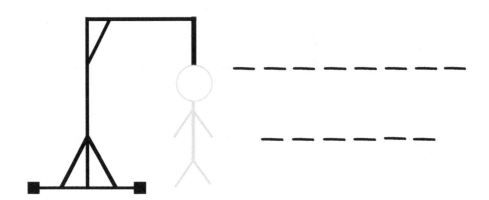

- - - - - - - - - - - - - - - -

- - - - - - - - - - - - -

A B C D E F G H I J K L M N O

P Q R S T U V W X Y Z

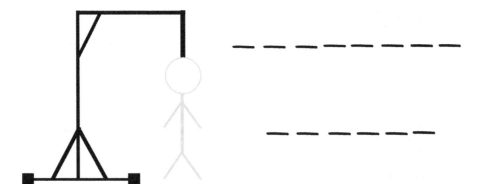

- - - - - - - - - - - - -

- - - - - -

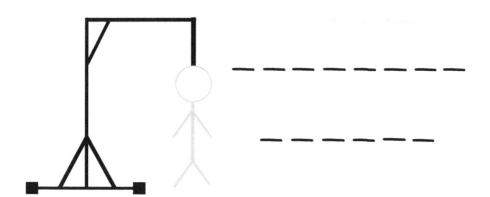

- - - - - - - - - - - - -

- - - - - - - -

A B C D E F G H I J K L M N O
P Q R S T U V W X Y Z

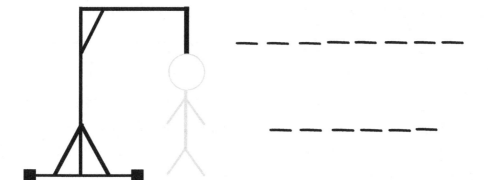

- - - - - - - - - -

- - - - - - -

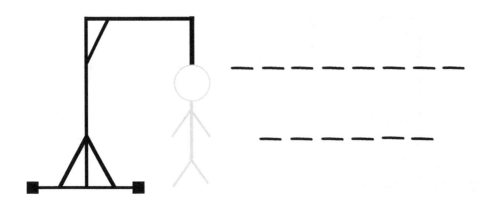

ABCDEFGHIJKLMNO
PQRSTUVWXYZ

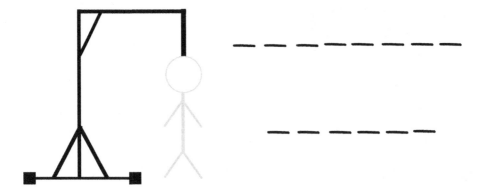

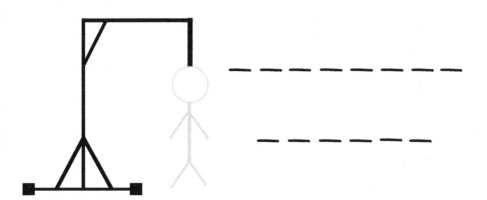

_ _ _ _ _ _ _ _ _

_ _ _ _ _ _

ABCDEFGHIJKLMNO
PQRSTUVWXYZ

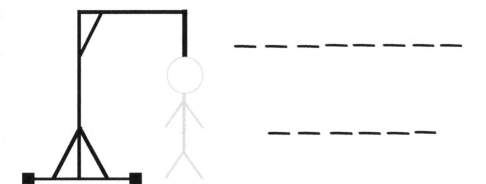

_ _ _ _ _ _ _ _ _

_ _ _ _ _ _

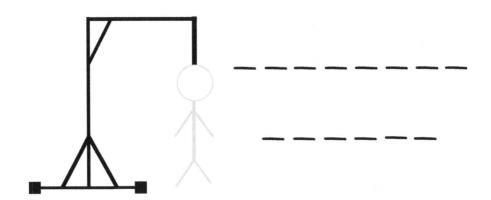

_ _ _ _ _ _ _ _ _

_ _ _ _ _ _ _

A B C D E F G H I J K L M N O

P Q R S T U V W X Y Z

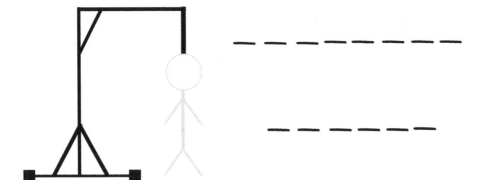

_ _ _ _ _ _ _ _ _

_ _ _ _ _ _ _

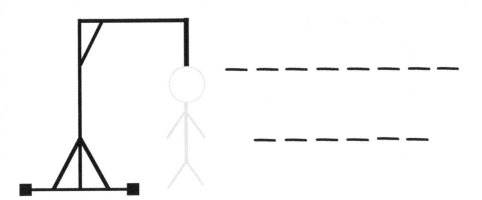

_ _ _ _ _ _ _ _ _ _ _

_ _ _ _ _ _ _

ABCDEFGHIJKLMNO

PQRSTUVWXYZ

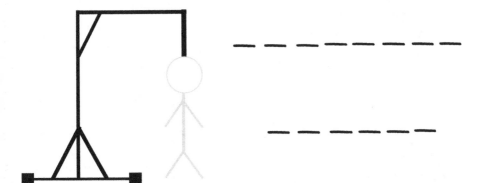

_ _ _ _ _ _ _ _ _ _

_ _ _ _ _ _ _

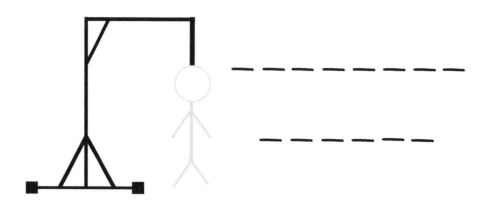

A B C D E F G H I J K L M N O

P Q R S T U V W X Y Z

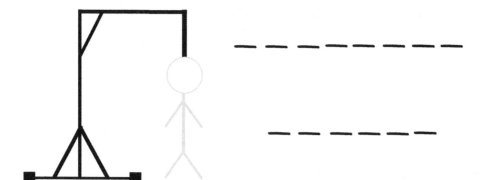

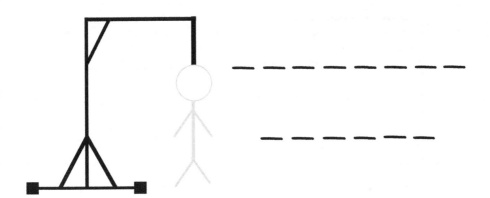

_ _ _ _ _ _ _ _ _ _ _ _

_ _ _ _ _ _ _ _

ABCDEFGHIJKLMNO

PQRSTUVWXYZ

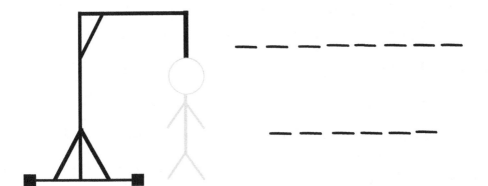

_ _ _ _ _ _ _ _ _ _ _ _

_ _ _ _ _ _ _ _

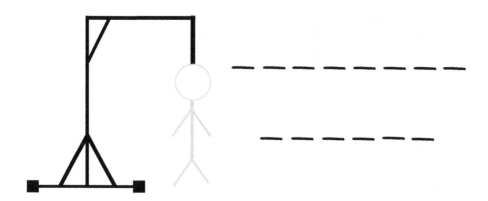

- - - - - - - - - - - - - - - - - -

- - - - - - - - - - - - - -

ABCDEFGHIJKLMNO
PQRSTUVWXYZ

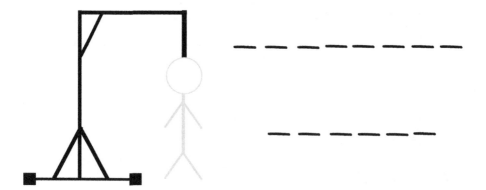

- - - - - - - - - - - - - - - - - -

- - - - - - - - - - - -

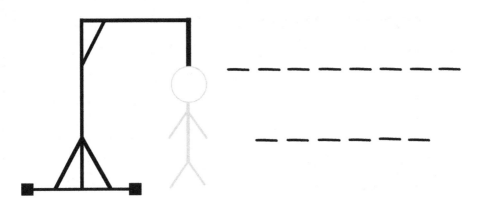

_ _ _ _ _ _ _ _ _

_ _ _ _ _ _

A B C D E F G H I J K L M N O
P Q R S T U V W X Y Z

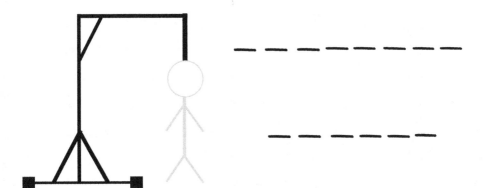

_ _ _ _ _ _ _ _ _

_ _ _ _ _ _

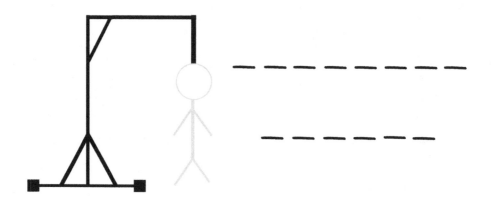

ABCDEFGHIJKLMNO

PQRSTUVWXYZ

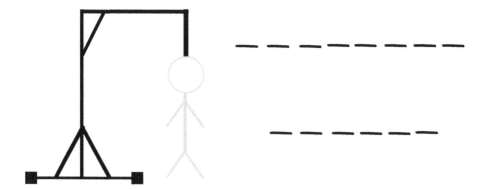

Made in the USA
Coppell, TX
01 October 2021